DOCTOR'S DREAMS

DR. COLONEL M SITARAM

INDIA • SINGAPORE • MALAYSIA

Copyright © M Sitaram 2023
All Rights Reserved.

ISBN 979-8-89026-676-7

This book has been published with all efforts taken to make the material error-free after the consent of the author. However, the author and the publisher do not assume and hereby disclaim any liability to any party for any loss, damage, or disruption caused by errors or omissions, whether such errors or omissions result from negligence, accident, or any other cause.

While every effort has been made to avoid any mistake or omission, this publication is being sold on the condition and understanding that neither the author nor the publishers or printers would be liable in any manner to any person by reason of any mistake or omission in this publication or for any action taken or omitted to be taken or advice rendered or accepted on the basis of this work. For any defect in printing or binding the publishers will be liable only to replace the defective copy by another copy of this work then available.

Dedication

I dedicate this book of poems to my father
(Late) Sri Manthripragada Ramarao Garu & my mother
(Late) Smt M Sitadevi, for making me what I am today!
I acknowledge the encouragement, support & help
from my entire family and colleagues who helped me
complete this project successfully.

CONTENTS

FOREWORD

I always wanted to be a Doctor from as far as I can recall, since it is one profession most respected and always rewarding! After more than 5 decades of professional career as a Physician, Cardiologist, Teacher and an Army doctor during wars & peace, I have a myriad memories of frequent encounters with Life, Sickness & Death from close quarters, embellished with colorful images of past travels all over the world. I wanted to share these impressions with others in the form of poems since a few lines of poetry can often transport the reader right in to the scene of action & convey more than a paragraph of prose. As William Wordsworth said "Poetry is the spontaneous overflow of powerful feelings, taking origin from emotions recollected in tranquillity!!" Hope you will enjoy reading the poems as much as I enjoyed penning them. Happy reading!

TABLE FOR TWO

It is Valentine's Day,
At the popular 'Cafe Latte',
And I have a table for two,
Just for Me & You!

Third year in college,
At last some spare time we manage,
To sip hot coffee & lick ice cream,
To slip in to a sweet reverie & enjoy a daydream!

In boring class room lectures on maxillary bones,
On endless discussions on kidney stones & abdominal
groans,
I was always looking at you,
And knew U were watching me too!

Nimble student fingers, on key boards flew,
(But some clever teachers, they always knew),
The urgent desire to share everything,
That desperate longing... for a planned evening!

The hint of fragrance in your bouncy hair,
That defiant laugh that said 'I don't care',
The subtle mischief of your parted lips,
You knew I worshipped you right to your fingertips!

As I wait here and watch the other couples,
I wonder if today is the last day of my troubles,
I think about the sweet nothings we shared,
All the little mystery gifts we traded!

Today I realised what I must do,
To prove to me & you that my love is true!
I must look in to your eyes and ask you to be mine,
For today, tomorrow and till the end of Time!

But wait, who is that guy walking in with you?
He is grinning so smugly and so are you!
A brief hand shake, a gold braided wedding card!
Left me standing speechless, just like a mental retard!!

If only my mind could speak & my heart could sing,
I wouldn't be so dependent on my idiotic tongue!
Nor would I need these stupid roses red,
I could've mailed you my ECG instead!

It is Valentine's Day,
At the popular 'Cafe Latte',
And I have a table for two,
Just for me & myself, yes, I do!

COLOURS IN CRITICAL CARE

As doctor in charge of Intensive Care,
Amidst patients & papers with little time to spare,
I dabble in poetry and doodle with my pencil,
But silence from the ECG monitors, has always been
My worst nightmare!

I sent my poems & a few lines of prose,
To pals in whose language skills, trust I repose.
"Nice English" they gushed, "But your work
Is all dark and too morose!"

But how can I compose,
Cute little rhymes,
While trying to fiddle with one hand,
The blessed IV Noradrenaline dose?

I stood at the bed, of a 10 yr old child,
(With Covid symptoms mild),
And watched as she did her homework, (with her mom as
her guide!)
The little flowers on her art book rapidly bloomed in
colour,
And a pretty rainbow appeared, as Mom & child broke into
smiles wide!

I looked out of the ICU window,
The rain had stopped, the sky had a hint of a Rainbow!
I knew Mother Nature was setting up a jolly good show!
I run out to the fire escape steps, and take off my mask!
For a few moments of fresh air & best view of world below!

There'll always be work & guidelines for duty,
But do spare a moment to savour,
Mother Nature's real beauty,
The colours of the world, will continue to amaze us,
Thank your Mentor above for lacing sickness & sadness
with laughter & gaiety!

THE LIFT

'Tenth floor' A silky voice croons,
As the doors smoothly slide apart.
I watch a few giggling Nurses enter,
Eager for a new day to start!

Eleventh floor, the doors open
To let in a man with his hand in a sling,
Obviously in severe pain, he clutches,
His wife's arm & stares at the ceiling!

A couple enter, at the next level, the twelfth,
They argue loudly, as if in a private room!
The lift shudders a bit, moans as it shakes back & forth,
Suddenly it stops with a violent jerk & a loud Boom!

A moment of silence, as everyone hold their breath,
Their differences forgotten, the pains wane away,
"Don't worry Dear," says the man with a sling,
As people huddle in the dark, their hands grope for
support,

A baritone voice starts to sing
 "Count your many blessings, name them one by one,
& It'll surprise you what the Lord has done!"
The lights come on, elevator starts to move,

Gently it descends with its precious cargo,
The smiles are back, giggling resumes,
The passengers walk out laughing and joking,
As they approach the coffee shop at Ground Floor!

HOWRAH BRIDGE

Watch your step, little brother.
The path is blocked by a boulder.
You need never worry or bother,
As long as you keep your hand on my shoulder!

There's a cool spot near the bridge,
I'll get you there by noon,
Just cross this final ridge,
I will help you sit down very soon!!

The Sun is hot & our lips are dry.
Looked for our father everywhere,
Do not despair, please don't cry
Keep walking, we are almost there!

Feel the rumble of the street,
As the bridge itself vibrates,
A thousand shuffling feet,
Yet no one who looks,
No one cares!

A mother is guiding, her children to school,
She adjusts their caps, waves them good bye,
I wish we had a mother, to feed us some food,
To tell us stories & hold us when we cry.

Just sit down in the shade,
Of this mighty steel monster,
Settle down, in the niche, I just for you made,
At the Howrah Bridge, a heartless wonder!

Do take out your little dented bowl,
Match your ballads with my finger drum beat,
Sing your heart out, let them hear your soul,
Hope they throw some coins, along with the dust of their
feet!

Baba is somewhere, walking with a banner coloured Red,
He shouts some slogans, just to earn us some bread!
He rests awhile under the statue, of the great Dr BC Roy,
As we huddle & sleep under the bridge, in this city of Joy!

MOTHER'S BROW

The lights on the porch are fully lit,
The mother at the window continues to sit,
She holds her phone close to her chest,
Her daughter's not home! No, not yet!

Shutters of the shops are slowly pulled down,
As tired workers return to homes downtown,
The rain has stopped, the streets are still wet,
Her daughter's not home! No, not just yet!

The night watchman, blows his short shrill whistle,
While the anxious mother keeps her lone long vigil.
The neighbours watch, they all know it.
Her daughter's not home. Oh no, not yet!

"I am nineteen, Mom, you are such a big bore!"
"Don't tell me about life, a little baby I am no more!"
Went off on a bike, with a guy she had just met,
Her daughter's not home. No, not just yet!

"Wait my child, I want to give you some tips"...,
But the bike went off roaring, even as the words were on
her lips!
"Be careful my baby, my words lest you forget…"
But the daughter's not home. No, not yet!

A lizard on the wall approaches her prey,
The mother closes her eyes, continues to pray,
Often, she spoke to her baby about strange men on the
'Net',
But the daughter's not home. No not yet!

The hands of the clock have got their rhythm right,
Tick-toking their dance towards their tryst at midnight,
Gave her child all her love as a single parent,
But the daughter's not home. No not yet!

I end this 'Ode to Mothers', with an ending uncertain,
As on this episode, I draw a slow curtain.

The welcome sounds of footsteps on her porch, are a balm
to the mother's brow.
Her heart beats faster, and her face is again aglow!
The sounds of muted laughter, as a biker waves and speeds
away!
A 'Mother and Child Reunion' is just a moment away!

FOOTSTEPS IN THE SAND

The distant lights blink to remind,
Of the desert camp we left behind.
With our sneakers held in our hand,
We feel with our feet, the cool desert sand.

"We stop here" our guide is quite firm,
He does a quick count, just to confirm.
"Folks, we go no further, for yonder,
Lies the Indo-Pak International border!"

We sit down, to have a swig of water,
My flask is gone, strangely it doesn't matter.
I look up at the sky & drink in the glorious sight,
The grand spectacle of a silent star-studded night!

A million diamonds for me, spread out on a tray,
There is Sirius, this one is Pluto, here's the Milky way!
All my friends from the skies, lost in the foggy city,
I had to travel miles to find you again, what a pity!

Stop the crackers, headlines scream,
Ban orders by the court supreme,
Can they be lightly dismissed?
Are they enough to restore, the clean air we miss?

"Get up, it's time to go!" The group leader dictates,
But to break a beautiful reverie he surely hesitates,
I pull myself up from the sand, from a dream sublime,
Shuffle back, leaving footsteps in the sands of Time!

THE YOUNG ONES

I remember them from those first classes,
The young boys with new moustaches,
Those pretty girls with their hair in curls,
And some with big eyes & outsized glasses!

Their eagerness knew no bounds,
As I taught them their first heart sounds.
From cautious forays to effortless ease,
They glided in to a pool of Medicine & Heart disease!

They spoke with candour,
About the inner fears they harbour,
Of their love for rides on mo-bikes,
And their numerous likes and dislikes!

In classrooms filled with endless chatter,
Labs & dissection halls that echoed their laughter,
They somehow picked up the professional ropes,
Amidst fears, anxieties, wonder and high hopes!

Dancing their way through studies, numerous tests,
Cultural shows, sports meets & cookery contests,
Eager to try a trendy look, lipstick, a new make up or two,
They encountered early love and painful break ups too!

Waving goodbye to college, friends & faculty,
The young docs plunge in to a world of reality,
A new life ahead and unknown challenges to face.
They line up for new plans, fresh targets, and a new race!

They wave at us through pictures now,
With their smiling spouses & kids in tow,
As new PGs and young specialists today,
They march to their new goals,
Each in their own special way!

FLIGHT TO DELHI

I saw a young soldier, at the airport today,
We spoke at the soda fountain at the far end of the hall.
His face was pensive and his hair was in disarray!
I enquired his name & destination, as we made small talk!

"Delhi" he said in low monotone.
 "My mother is unwell.
Her neighbours called,
She has lost her voice, can't move her hand!

She fell down at her home
And her collar bone also broke!
The doctors are quite puzzled,
They suspect a massive stroke!"

"I am posted high up in the hills,
At home there's no help, no one to care,
I fear for her life, & the huge medical bills,
As she fights her lone battle in ICU somewhere!"

"Calling all passengers to Delhi, at counter no 9"
A sing song voice calls out and the crowd scrambles to get
in line,
There's confusion tonight,
As this is an overbooked flight!

The soldier with his duffel bag is asked to stand aside,
His status not confirmed, he turns back, biting his lips!
As the rest of the laughing crowd prepares to board the
flight.
I feel my heart tug, at my soldier friend's plight.

I walked up to the soldier,
His eyes were closed very tight,
As he finished his silent prayer, I put my hand on his
shoulder.
"Don't worry, my friend! You will definitely fly tonight!"

I approached the booking counter,
To ask for a cancellation,
Made a request! "Could they please make a concession,
Take the young army jawan, instead?"

The lady at the desk, smiles at me,
"Thank you kind Sir,
We have six men already making way,
For that one passenger!

Good News, for all of you,
We shall be taking everyone!
Got your friend a seat next to you,
He'd feel better, talking one to one!"

As the flight takes off, gaining altitude,
My new found pal, reclines his seat,
Looks at me with gratitude.
As his eyes brim with tears,
I stop him, from touching my feet!

THE CHOCOLATE FOUNTAIN

Let's meet in the Mall at the chocolate fountain,
Today, say sometime 'tween six and six-ten.
We'll turn the clock back, (let's at least try),
To the days, months and the years that went by!

Those dangling earrings you gently picked,
As I grabbed the moment in my lens and clicked.
The silky hair that fell all over your face
As we ran 'tween the shops,
In a mock lemon and spoon race!

My stupid jokes, your deep throaty laughter,
That stayed with me long into the morning
..and then, ever after!
I wish I had more money, you said you had no more time!
But to let those precious moments go by,
would've been such a stupid crime!

Sadly, we had to part one day,
Both of us, to go on our own way.
But you read my tweets, said they made you cry,
I knew photos may fade, but memories ..they never die!

Let's meet in the mall at the chocolate fountain,
Today say sometime 'tween six & six ten,
Will turn the clock back (at least let's try),
to the days and months and years that went by!

FIRST DAY IN SCHOOL

I sit up in bed, rubbing my eyes,
My wife is restless, unable to sleep.
She gets up once more to sip some water,
While our little son is curled up in bed, his comic books in
a big heap!

The week that went by, was a mad hectic rush,
From one corner to another, we ran around the town,
It was a new academic term, and it was time,
To find for our little one, a school to call his own!

A Crowd of anxious parents jostles,
On sidewalks that sold school bags for a song,
And street corners, selling pencils and water bottles!
But at shops selling notebooks, the lines were pretty long!

The big day arrived with a bang,
My son was escorted to the school gate by his mom,
She spent the whole morning, ringing her hands in despair,
Looking at the clock every few minutes!

"Hope my little one had a good seat,
Wonder if he had his lunch on time,
What if his new shoes pinch, and hurt his little feet!"
The mother's eyes are brimming with tears (and so are
mine)!

We run to the school bus, as it comes to a stop,
Home comes the hero, from his first day in school,
After a brief hug with his mom,
He is rolling on the floor with our dog!

"How was your first day" we were eager to know,
"What did they teach, did they make you stand in the sun?"
"No classes Mom. A little boy got a piece of chalk stuck in
his nose,
So we played the whole day and had lots of fun!"

A SYRINGEFUL OF SLEEP

The white lights forever remain bright,
From the irritating noises, there's no respite.
My 2nd day in the ICU, but things are not yet right,
Trying to catch some sleep, at least (a little) tonight!

The monitors with their lights blinking,
The nurses busy with their note scribbling,
I am just a troublesome patient in the second bed.
About my pain, no one has any inkling!

The computers hum, the printer chatters,
While doctors & helpers loudly discuss petty matters,
"Please let me SLEEP", I want to shout at the top of my
voice,
The stillness of the night, lies torn to many tatters!

Today, I am just a patient, in a stained hospital gown,
Not long ago, I had a decent life, all my very own!
I had my family, and had many a sweet dream!
Why am I so sick today, from this malady unknown?

The patient in my next bed, is in coma very deep.
I watch his family, sit around & silently weep.
It is so sad & funny that we all take health for granted,
It's like boasting that "I can sleep whenever I wanted!"

My mind goes in for a quick retrospect,
I've been a good man, of frugal habits, nothing suspect.
For medical profession I had nothing but respect,
Was I wrong then, if good health in return I expect?

The ECG monitors keep up their asynchronous beep,
While a vigil on erratic heartbeats they keep,
I have already counted a billion-blooming sheep,
But my mind is denied even a few winks of blissful sleep!

The kind duty doctor comes to my bed for a quick peep,
He adjusts my oxygen and asks me to breath deep,
"Give him a shot of Midazolam" he orders the nurse.
Aah, Good-night everyone,
Here comes the sister with a syringeful of sleep!

MONSOON IN THE HILLS

There's thunder overhead,
The sleet is tapping at my window,
It's time to close my laptop,
And head for the hills and the meadows!

We pack our bags, the rain gear,
Don our jackets and the rubber footwear.
As we lock our home to step out,
There's a flash of lightening, as if to show us the way!

The long train ride to the foothills,
The eager wait for the bus trip,
The scramble for the window seats,
A hot cup of Tea before we set off on our holiday!

The roads are shiny wet,
After the downpour last night.
There's a touch of dampness
In the cool air we inhale!

The slow ride uphill,
With hairpin bends everywhere,
Dew drops on the window sill,
That keep running here & there!

That lovely mansion in the hills,
It's going to be our homestay for this week,
Our link to nature, the birds & the bees!
We shall sing our favourite film songs,
As we lean out of the windows tonight!

A MOUSE IN MY HOUSE

My wife is standing on a sofa, Her hair in a tight bun!
She's holding a broomstick, brandishing it like a gun!
"Don't take off your shoes!" She screams in obvious panic!
"There's a mouse on the loose! We have to go out for
lunch!"
The fried rice was cooked well, by the chef at the local club,

But the thoughts on our mind,
Were on the mouse we left behind!
'Did we close the cupboards real tight?
Was the bookshelf door airtight?
What if the wily rodent,
Decides to dance on the Piano at night?'

We return to our home at 3PM,
Tip toe to the front door for a quick peep,
Alert to any sound or squeak,
I turn the key to enter my home!

Things appear quiet, as we enter,
No sign yet, of our unwelcome guest!
My wife walks in to the kitchen,
And faints as she views the havoc caused by the pest!

There's rice all over the floor!
The sugar bowl is upside down!
There's Coffee in the sink,
With tiny foot prints dirty brown!

I run to check my writing desk,,
If everything is in it's place!
Heave a sigh of relief, but wait!
Where's the Gold cap of favourite pen?

I rush to call the pest control,
But the phone was dead!
I found the cable was cut,
So, I decide to run instead!

There's a long queue at the pest control desk,
At the counter I was blabbering about invasion by the rats,
The manner my home turned upside down,
Asked for urgent help to catch the brats!

My eyes fell on a banner behind the desk,
About a huge reward for info about a missing white mouse,
That escaped the science labs of the city!
The white rodent, was quite well endowed with special genes,
Adept in computer languages, It also had a penchant for poetry, they said!

I was excited as I rushed home, To tell my spouse, not to
cry,
We were in luck, we'll trap this guy,
We'll laugh all the way to the bank, and next day we fly!!

..(Squeak,.Squeak, Mike Testing!)
Sorry folks, the Poem ends here,
The couple ran away after I bit them,
This is Dicky Mouse, signing off, Hoped, you liked my
Epitaph!

FATHER HAS A FALL

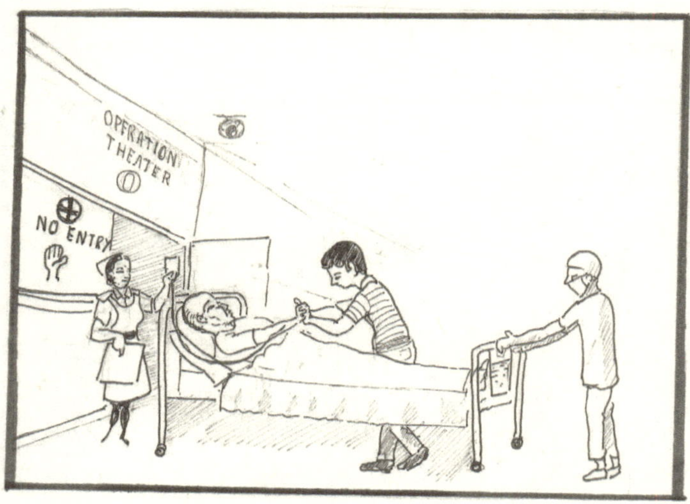

A bright & sunny day,
Sometime in mid-May,
My kids were smiling,
As we set off,
On our long-awaited Holiday!

The Flight to Nepal,
Was delayed, they said,
As we waited at the Airport,
To have a few cokes & some bread!

We hardly heard the mobile phone ring,
But my wife picked up the call,
Her face was sober as she said,
"Let us go back, Daddy just had a fall!"

The return trip by cab was silent,
But for the grating sound of my teeth,
My father was only eighty,
Why does he walk everywhere, and knock himself over?

We found him in bed,
With our servant standing by.
Dad smiled at us, through the pain,
And my anger slowly started to wane!

The doctor at the hospital said,
We were lucky got him in time,
The hip bone got broken,
And his BP was pretty high!

As they wheeled him to surgery,
They made me sign a few forms,
Father took my hand, said he was sorry!
Something tore inside me and I started to cry!

In the waiting room with a few visitors,
I was sobbing away, wiping my tears,
Someone brought me some water,
A grey haired gentleman hugged me!

It was the same hospital, same chairs,
My dad had brought me as a kid,
For injuries, sickness & growing pains,
Always consoled me, stood by my side,
How could I get annoyed with him in his frail old age?

Soon the surgery was done,
The smiling doctor shook my hand and led me inside,
Dad was groggy but opened his eyes,
He enquired about his grandchildren,
And I knew everything else was just fine!

NIGHT IN LONDON

We landed in London
On a warm afternoon,
Just another Indian couple,
On their eager honeymoon!

Our oversized bags,
Attracted many a smile,
Till we got stuck badly,
At the airport turnstile!

"What a lovely weather!"
I spoke to the turbaned cab driver,
He gave me a cold stare,
Perhaps I spoke too soon!

The long ride from Heathrow,
Is still fresh in my brain,
As we reached our hotel,
Through thick traffic & pouring rain!

We spent the next day,
Staring at the street below,
Obscured by thick London Fog,
From our hotel suite window!

"Catch a red double decker bus,
"It'll take you round the city"
The girl at the desk told us,
"A storm has come up, Oh, what a pity!"

We made it to the London Bridge,
Standing still upright,
Despite what they taught us
In those dark nursery rhymes,

The Castle Tower next door,
Still draws crowds!
But about the tales of the Crows,
I still have some serious doubts.

I bowed to Her Majesty, The Queen with her Crown,
While Prince Charles looked at us,
With what looked like a frown,
Diana, the princess was chatting in another corner,
At the Wax Museum of Madame Tussaud!

We went on a ride on the famous London Eye,
The block of buildings over there is the Westminster,
The chimes from the Big Ben are of course,
From the clock tower standing right below!

"This, Ladies & Gentlemen, is the historic Trafalgar square,
The Gentleman on the horse is of course, Lord Nelson
A few hundred yards down the road,
The famous Downing Street, Number 10!"

We stood outside the Palace Buckingham,
And watched the smart Guards ride their white horses,
While crowds clapped and clicked,
To carry home, their memories of London town!

We went in search of Sherlock Holmes, the famous sleuth!
And found his statue, next to a public phone booth!
Stood for a moment to salute my hero,
To recall his genius and logic in solving the toughest crimes
ever!

I stepped into the empty Lord's Cricket ground,
Walked to the Indian Team dressing room, full of nostalgia,
And stopped at a giant wall poster of Sachin Tendulkar on
the stairway!
As memories of all the famous test matches, came rushing
in to blow me away!

How can we miss, the famous London Metro,
A maze of tunnels underground!
I recall the Luftwaffe night bombings,
While the people huddled in bunkers below!

We dressed up in the evening, in colourful raincoats,
Eager to go shopping, in the spacious London malls!
"Sorry Sir, But didn't you read the sign board behind?
Everything here, except the pubs, close early at Five!"

I wanted to roam the streets to meet,
James Bond (007), Jeeves the butler, and the Beatles singing
on the street,
And I would love to have a few selfie clicks,
With Harry Potter with his magic tricks!

Tomorrow, we leave, early in the day,
On the next leg of our adventure,
Another city, for another foray!
Would love to visit London again,
perhaps on a bright sunny day!

GOLD FISH LESSONS

The eastern sky had just turned pinkish grey,
The early morning Sun was preparing to send out his first rays,
I hear a faint sobbing sound outside my bedroom door,
Enter the kid's room to find my little daughter weeping!

Her cheeks were wet with tears
"It's my Goldfish daddy,
He's stopped moving since last night
But floating upside down!"

I took the fish bowl down,
Sat down to hug my child!
Spoke to her softly for a while,
As I wiped her nose & held her close.

How do I explain to you my child,
Every creature has a time,
That nothing lasts forever,
However pretty, however sublime!

I took her out for a walk in the garden,
Among the blooming flowers smiling in their beds,
While the dead leaves & withered flowers,
Were being raked away in a small corner!

Nature has a way to recycle life,
To recreate magic, after the colours fade away,
More living wonders are waiting in line,
To come & play their part in a drama without an ending!

That evening, I rearranged her room,
The window blinds have bright butterflies,
Her Fish bowl has a baby tortoise swimming about,
And a flower pot with a single sapling eager to grow!

NIGHT FLIGHT TO VENUS

I opened my eyes, the sheets thrown aside.
It was only a dream, a sleepy cerebrum's nocturnal ride.
The handsome Prince was only a hallucination.
His white stallion, a figment of mere imagination.

Over the glades, across the meadows we had bounded.
We shouted, we shrieked, our laughter in hills resounded!
Our thoughts came across in torrents, the words swirled in
rivulets!
The distant stars were no match for the sparkling stars on
his epaulets.

We spoke of his postings, his love for music and painting.
He smiled at my scraggy hair, my undying passion for
dancing.
We gazed at each other in silence, as if speech itself was an
intrusion.
Was this 'Real love' I wondered, or was it just a colourful
illusion?

It was time to leave. A time to say goodbye.
I turned my face as I wipe the tears in my eye.
"Wait for me, I'll come back real quick" he said,
Kissed me gently as he led me back to my bed.

Now I cannot wait any longer. Hope the day ends soon.
I have a date in my room, my only witness, the full moon,
Eager to go back to dreams and my Prince Charming,
For my 'Night Flight to Venus'& do not disturb me till
morning.

THE LAST POST

The world is in slumber deep
Yet the woman was unable to sleep!
Her husband is in the army,
Somewhere on his lonely duty!

She had spoken to her Soldier, just a week back,
Laughed into the unsteady line,
"We are all doing fine!
Just come back at harvest time!"

She did not dare tell him,
About her little child unwell with high fever,
The flood waters that surround the village,
Threatening to enter her home!

The power lines snap,
The wind howls an unholy tune,
And dark clouds gather,
To blot the little light of the moon!

She lights a small lamp,
At the picture on the mantle,
To close her eyes in prayer,
As the flame flickers in the wind!

She pictures her husband,
Guarding her great Nation
At the last border outpost,
High on a snowbound mountain!

She knows of the solemn Oath he had taken,
Of placing "Duty before Self, The 'Country' before 'Family',
His Task before his comfort,
Every time and all the Time!"

She bows down her head in prayer,
For her spouse at the border,
Like a million army wives,
Who understand the Nation's Needs!

Let us all take a pledge,
To salute the Indian Armed Forces,
It's unsung heroes, the unsung valour,
And the unseen families behind them!

AN EVENING IN PARIS

The 'Eurostar' bullet train glides in,
Gently stops with a hiss,
I step down to the platform, to take in,
My very first breath in the famed city of Paris!

Crossing the English Channel, was easy as a breeze,
Sitting in the seat of a luxury train!
Wish it was half as easy for the allied soldiers of yore,
Who died crossing the channel at Normandy!

Crossing the streets, with crowds young & old,
Who speak and cheer in dialects unknown,
I recall the books, mysteries,
And so many romances untold!

We line up at the Museum 'Lovre'
For a view of the famous painting of Mona Lisa.
I jostle with crowds to gaze at the smiling visage.
Across the myriads of raised hands with mobile cams,

She looks back at me, imploring with eyes forlorn.
"Free me from this glass cage, From this stuffy room full of
lights!
Take me home, from this crowd,
I want to sleep in silence and darkness tonight!"

I drag myself away,
From the smiling lady, and her secrets,
To find solace in the creations
of Vincent Von Gogh.
Stand speechless at the gallery showing
Marble sculptures of a bygone era!
Those silken veils of fair maiden,
And the scraggy faces of slaves

I watch the setting Sun, turning red,
As I stroll among trees decked with lights to watch
A marching band play the drums, while the crowds sing
along,
Stare at the Arc d'Tromphe looking resplendent, decked up
for the night!

The styles & high Fashion of Paris,
On display again tonight,(? De Ja Vu)
As a swinging crowd breaks into a dance impromptu,
The sidewalk cafes spring to life!
Well heeled Gentlemen alight from their Porches & Mercs,
High heeled ladies click their tall Champaigne glasses at
Champs Ellysee!

The waiters dart deftly among tables,
 Laid out on the kerb with their trays & glasses.
Sounds of Music & gay laughter announce,
Yet another Parisian evening has just begun.

I take a boat ride down the river Seine,
Under bridges of fine marble,
With statues of Nymphets rarely seen!
The banks lined up with couples in deep romance!

The horizon is full of churches & spires,
But my eyes scan for the one church described by Sir Victor
Hugo ,
The pretty scenery floats by,then I see it, the burnt out
remains
Of the famous Church of Notre Dame!

I climbed the Eiffel Tower
On my last day in Paris,
Stood there waving for a moment,
Did I hear the City call out, "Come back in July for Bastille
Day,
RSVP (Respondez S'il Vous Plait)"

TAJ MAHAL

We push through the crowds, the odours and the noises around us.
A visit to Agra, the next item on the 'Visit India' itinerary tonight!
A glimpse of the Taj Mahal, a rare treat for us, the 'outsiders'!
I hold my wife's hand tighter as I didn't want to lose her,
In the fading evening light!

As we enter the courtyard, my heart skips a beat!
I stand speechless, rooted to the ground,
Unmindful of the crowds, the oppressive heat,
Gazing in awe, at the splendour of the monument around!

The Doc who talks of nothing
But the heart & cardiac murmurs,
Can he ever understand anything,
About this poetry penned in Sang-e-murmur?

Oh Yes, I do! I know of heart aches,
All about burning love and sleepless nights!
And I salute the courage it takes,
To say sorry after those petty little fights!

But to build a towering marble edifice,
To your favourite 'Begum', I concede,
Neither money nor power alone suffice!
A true romantic, always does succeed!

A ROOM WITH A VIEW

"Here we are", the Matron said,
"Room number 502,
I understand you insisted,
On having a room with a good view!"

"You can see the Diamond Harbour from here,
And smell the fish as the tide comes in,
The New Market junction is quite near,
But the local trams & buses do make a huge din!"

"Here at Alcoholics Anonymous"
She continued,
"We are quite open minded.
But a big NO..NO to drugs, and I hope you are not carrying
any booze"

Joseph is coming up with your luggage,
He will help you unpack!
We will see you at Dinner by the poolside in half an hour,
Do wear a shirt with an open collar!

Joseph, was an old hand at the place,
He winked at me & laid out my dress,
"Can slip in Rum Old Monk, any time of the day,
But for a Single Malt Whiskey, I would need cash in
advance!"

I gazed out of the window at the sea,
And heard the tugboats toot their horns below,
The blinking lights of the distant ships,
Seemed to be beaming a message straight at me!

Sandhya, was standing at the window, with hands on her
hips
Her hair gently catching the breeze!
"How did you..?" My query never left my lips,
She slowly turned to face me and fix me in her gaze,
"Why did you lie to me?" her soft voice was laced half in
anguish and half in anger.

I slumped down in to a chair,
Recoiling from the sudden onslaught!
"It's been 15 years, Sandhya! We were just teenagers"
"Why did you lie to me?" Her voice was choked!
I put my head in my hands, When I looked up she was
gone!

Dinner was a damp affair,
Lots of elderly men.
Hoping to slip by unseen,
Among a few ladies middle aged, & a couple in their teens!.

Tepid tasteless soup, followed by endless banter,
About Alcohol & it's evil sway,
Despite the power of the mind over matter!
We broke up at ten, with plans for a psychology lecture next
day!

After a fitful sleep and tossing about in bed,
I found I had company, my dad was sitting in the chair,
He left us long ago, I had given him up for dead!
He looked pale as a ghost, with flowing beard of grey hair!

"Why did you leave mom & me?" I asked him,
As he looked out of the window, mumbled about something
I couldn't fathom!
"They threw us out, Dad! Burnt our house down!
My friends, they mocked me,
I needed you bad!"

He walked away as silently as he entered,
Melted in to the shadows behind the curtains,
Left me restless, bewildered!
As I pinched myself to know if I was in my senses!

Right after yoga class next day,
They made us sit in a circle,
One by one my friends spoke,
Of their life, and their failures while a few just walked away!

I told them about my life, my dreams,
My plans of a working with the film stars,
As I sipped beer with pals from my 'hood!
Of Love, early heart breaks and the fights in the bars!

Psychology lectures that followed,
Were not too bad, we agreed!
They told us to stay firm,
Resist temptation & beware of Hallucinations!

Sandhya was in my room again at night,
Sitting cross legged on the window sill,
She had a lit cigarette in hand,
Blowing smoke rings in to the night sky!

"Be careful" I shouted, as she leaned forward,
To dangle her dainty ankles in to the night sky.
"Come & catch me!" She taunted as she slipped out,
As I rushed to grab her, I clutched at empty air and found
myself falling!

DISNEY WORLD

The schools are closed for vacation,
My grandson is restless, as the holidays go by,
The parents are busy with their vocation,
It's left for me to plan an outing, to keep the kid occupied!

We set off to visit the world of Disney,
Where childhood fantasies always come alive!
I remember my first encounters at Disney's,
And hoped the kid & Grandpa can bring the magic back to life!

The day was bright & sunny as we punch in our tickets,
Squeals of delight from happy children as we pass the gates.
Myriad visual scenes unfold before us, as we enter,
To turn the clock back to happy childhood days!

There's Mickey Mouse in his top hat,
Minnie with fancy ribbons in her hair,
There's Goofy, trying hard to pedal his bike,
And Donald Duck the hero, struts about in his waddling
gait!

We run along to the pier to see a pirate ship set sail,
With a pennant of skull & cross bones, flying on the high
mast.
The Dolphins are playing beach ball in the shallows,
While the Crocodiles were on a tea break!

The wicked sisters of Cinderella are there, picking their
gowns,
As the cunning step mother plans to woo the prince & the
crown!
High walls around the castle can never stop the music in
the air,
The Glass coach is ready to take Cinderella back at
midnight.
Aah, Life is so unfair!

We rode the big paddle boat, right across the lake,
Where sharks and whales were jostling for space,
And sailed in the jungle waterways, in a canoe
While Red Indians were shooting arrows at the settlers.

We went up the mountain, on a bone rattling ride,
Came screaming down splashing over the water slide!
Put on coloured 3D glasses, to watch roaring dinosaurs,
Lost our way in an endless mirrored maze!

"Are they all real Grandpa?" I paused as I tried to answer
the question back at home.
"Yes, little one, I think they are" was the best response,
I could give.
As I turned to switch off the light,
And put him to bed that night,
I glanced at the scribbled entry in his little diary,
"I shook hands with Donald Duck today!" it said!

MY PERSONAL ANGEL

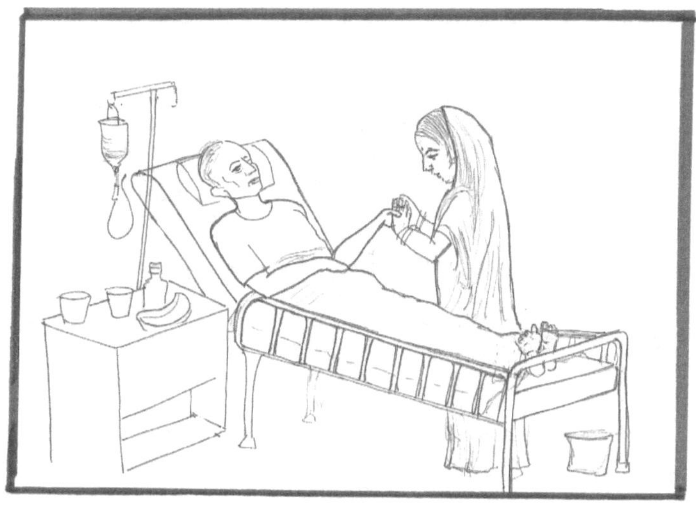

The marathon operation is over, at last.
"How is he doing?" My voice quivers as I ask.
The surgeon's eyes are unusually grim
As he speaks in jargon, of prognosis very dim!

The drugs and the dressings are of simply no use,
To give you some solace, from a cancer so diffuse!
So frail, so lonely, you looked forlorn in bed.
"Were you crying?" you whispered. I just shook my head.

Look at me, my Darling, don't sleep so soon,
I wore that blue dress, you gave me last June!
We need to talk, I need more time,
I want to tell you 'I love you', as I hold your hands in mine!

A thousand emotions cloud my anxious brain,
As I watch you smile, through your endless pain!
You, my Dear, gave me so much in life,
Do me a favor, give me all your pain, I am your wife!

The end of the road is approaching so fast,
I would've given anything to make it forever last!
Sadly I watch, , the world around me crumble,
"Farewell, My Darling" was all that I could mumble!

The world still goes on, even though you are no more,
The house is so empty despite memories galore.
Your room has been locked up, that day ever since,
I have to go in to clean up, my mind I convince.

I turn in the key, to step through the door,
I flick on the light switch, it is dark no more!
I sense it, I know it, I am certain you are there,
My eyes can't fool me, you are up there somewhere

I know my personal angel over me is watching,
I hope he is in peace, and forever keeps smiling,
In a world sans sickness, sans medicines,
Somewhere in the skies, in a land of happiness & only
happiness!

SIKKIM SAGA

The touchdown was smooth as silk,
As we landed at Bagdogra airport, on our maiden trip,
To Sikkim, the land of Honey & Milk,
That's what the hoardings said!

We stopped to take a deep breath,
At the top of the ladder steps,
To catch our first sight,
of the majestic 'Kanchenjunga'
Just a distant mountain delight!

We drove for the next 4 hours,
On winding mountain roads,
Passing convoys of soldiers,
Heading for distant frontiers.

'Welcome to Sikkim',
The simple sign post proclaimed,
At the state border check post,
where we halted to check our ID

Sikkim was a Himalayan Kingdom,
with zero reported crime, till
The merger with the Indian Union,
The rest they say is History!

Teesta, The mighty river, leaps & bounds in joy,
Gurgling alongside the winding roads,
A tiny rivulet during summer,
But come monsoon, the waters,
sound like an angry Lion's roar!

'Rangpo', a colourful little town
Was our very first stop,
To sip cold mineral water, and
Purchase a gallon of local Rum!

The green rolling hills are tea plantations,
And the distant snow peaks,
Are the Himalayan Mountains,
The true guardians of the Indian Nation!

A visit to the hilltop monastery,
At the famous school of 'Rumtek',
Was the next stop on the agenda,
But we rest tonight on soft sheets,
With Chinese Dragon designs!

We step in to the prayer hall of the monastery,
Our footwear respectfully parked outside,
Our eyes take time to adjust,
To the flickering light from a hundred tiny flames,

The buzz of a hundred chanted prayers,
The soft aroma of burning incense
And the huge towering Budha himself,
So serene in his lotus pose!

Each street in Gangtok lies on a steep slope,
Do not slip or you'll land up at the place where you started!
Fair skinned damsels, demure in their 'Bukkoh',
Smile as you roll by,
Hands full of shopping bags, clutching the camera for your
dear life!

The Dragon motif is everywhere,
The plates, curtains and the signboards,
Surely you must buy,
The exotic local jewellery as a gift,
The famous 'Gangtok Dragon Set'!

The streets are full of local folks,
The young bearing headloads,
As the elders spin their prayer wheels!
Their smiling faces full of wrinkles!

If you love the sunset colours,
You must visit North Sikkim,
Walk down the valley of Flowers,
As the prayer flags flutter in the wind to say,
"Om Mani Padme Hum"!

SUMMER HOLIDAY

After the deadly dances of virus COVID,
And the sizzling days of Summer torrid,
The mind yearns for a holiday,
And the body deserves a break!

Time to take out the maps,
As we make plans afresh, to discover new lands.
The islands of Lakshadweep silently beckoned us,
To a quiet holiday away from phones,TV and screaming
headlines

The holiday was very short,
Yet left behind memories sweet & long.
Discovered no Gold on the island named 'Bangaram' ...
But I found something much more valuable!

In a quiet Isle encircled by deep blue sea,
A gentle aura..a sense of inner peace!
Among the gentle laps of the waves and the cry of the
seagulls,
We discovered euphoria beyond measure!

The cool white sand beneath the soles of our feet,
The distant horizons where sky and ocean meet,
The tangy odour sea breeze everywhere,
Reminded of our childhood past.

The freedom from phones, TV and the net,
The liberty from being tied down to appointments to be met.
This is luxury in nature's lap!
This is what we miss in TV and WhatsApp!!

The sketches in the book are drawn by the Author himself.

Thanks to Notion Press Publishers.